family favorites
vegetables

Bath · New York · Singapore · Hong Kong · Cologne · Delhi · Melbourne

eggplant dip

ingredients

SERVES 6–8

1 large eggplant,
    about 14 oz/400 g

olive oil

2 scallions, chopped finely

1 large garlic clove, crushed

2 tbsp finely chopped fresh
    parsley

salt and pepper

smoked sweet Spanish paprika,
    to garnish

French bread, to serve

method

1 Cut the eggplant into thick slices and sprinkle with salt to draw out any bitterness; set aside for 30 minutes, then rinse and pat dry.

2 Heat 4 tablespoons of the oil in a large skillet over medium-high heat. Add the eggplant slices and cook on both sides until soft and starting to brown. Remove from the skillet and set aside to cool. The slices will release the oil again as they cool.

3 Heat another tablespoon of oil in the skillet. Add the onions and garlic and cook for 3 minutes until the scallions become soft. Remove from the heat and set aside with the eggplant slices to cool.

4 Transfer all the ingredients to a food processor and process just until a coarse purée forms. Transfer to a serving bowl and stir in the parsley. Taste and adjust the seasoning, if necessary. Serve at once, or cover and let chill until 15 minutes before required. Sprinkle with paprika and serve with slices of French bread.

zucchini fritters with yogurt dip

ingredients

SERVES 4

2–3 zucchini, about 14 oz/400 g

1 garlic clove, crushed

3 scallions, finely sliced

$4^1/2$ oz/125 g feta cheese
    (drained weight), crumbled

2 tbsp finely chopped
    fresh parsley

2 tbsp finely chopped
    fresh mint

1 tbsp finely chopped fresh dill

$1/2$ tsp freshly grated nutmeg

2 tbsp all-purpose flour

pepper

2 eggs

2 tbsp olive oil

1 lemon, cut into quarters,
    to garnish

for the dip

scant $1^1/4$ cups strained
    plain yogurt

$1/4$ cucumber, diced

1 tbsp finely chopped fresh dill

pepper

method

1 Grate the zucchini straight on to a clean dish towel and cover with another. Pat well and let stand for 10 minutes until the zucchini are dry.

2 Meanwhile, to make the dip, mix the yogurt, cucumber, dill, and pepper to taste in a serving bowl. Cover and let chill.

3 Tip the zucchini into a large bowl. Stir in the garlic, scallions, cheese, herbs, nutmeg, flour, and pepper to taste. Beat the eggs in a separate bowl and stir into the zucchini batter—the batter will be quite lumpy and uneven but this is fine.

4 Heat the oil in a large, wide pan over medium heat. Drop 4 tablespoonfuls of the batter into the skillet, with space in between, and cook for 2–3 minutes on each side. Remove, drain on paper towels, and keep warm. Cook the second batch of fritters in the same way. (There should be 8 fritters in total.)

5 Serve the fritters hot with the dip, garnished with lemon quarters.

vegetable soup with pistou

ingredients

SERVES 4

4 cups fresh cold water

bouquet garni of 1 fresh parsley
    sprig, 1 fresh thyme sprig,
    and 1 bay leaf, tied together
    with clean string

2 celery stalks, chopped

3 baby leeks, chopped

4 baby carrots, chopped

5 1/2 oz/150 g new potatoes,
    scrubbed and cut into
    bite-size chunks

4 tbsp shelled fava beans
    or peas

6 oz/175 g canned cannellini
    or flageolet beans, drained
    and rinsed

3 heads bok choy

scant 3 3/8 cups arugula

pepper

for the pistou

2 large handfuls fresh basil
    leaves

1 fresh green chili, seeded

2 garlic cloves

4 tbsp olive oil

1 tsp Parmesan cheese,
    finely grated

method

1 Put the water and bouquet garni into a large pan and add the celery, leeks, carrots, and potatoes. Bring to a boil, then reduce the heat and let simmer for 10 minutes.

2 Stir in the fava beans or peas and canned beans and let simmer for an additional 10 minutes. Stir in the bok choy, arugula, and pepper to taste and let simmer for an additional 2–3 minutes. Remove and discard the bouquet garni.

3 Meanwhile, to make the pistou, put the basil, chili, garlic, and oil into a food processor and pulse to form a thick paste. Stir in the cheese.

4 Stir most of the pistou into the soup, then ladle into warmed bowls. Top with the remaining pistou and serve at once.

sauteed garlic mushrooms

ingredients

**SERVES 6
AS PART OF A TAPAS
MEAL**

1 lb/450 g white mushrooms

5 tbsp Spanish olive oil

2 garlic cloves, finely chopped

squeeze of lemon juice

salt and pepper

4 tbsp chopped fresh
   flat-leaf parsley

crusty bread, to serve

method

1 Wipe or brush clean the mushrooms, then trim off the stalks close to the caps. Cut any large mushrooms in half or into quarters. Heat the olive oil in a large, heavy-bottom skillet, add the garlic and cook for 30 seconds–1 minute, or until lightly browned. Add the mushrooms and sauté over high heat, stirring most of the time, until the mushrooms have absorbed all the oil in the skillet.

2 Reduce the heat to low. When the juices have come out of the mushrooms, increase the heat again, and sauté for 4–5 minutes, stirring most of the time, until the juices have almost evaporated. Add a squeeze of lemon juice and season to taste with salt and pepper. Stir in the parsley and cook for an additional minute.

3 Transfer the sautéed mushrooms to a warmed serving dish and serve piping hot or warm. Accompany with chunks or slices of crusty bread for mopping up the garlic cooking juices.

asparagus with melted butter

ingredients

SERVES 2

16–20 stalks of asparagus, trimmed to about 8 inches/20 cm

3 oz/85 g unsalted butter, melted

sea salt and pepper, to serve

method

1 Remove some of the base of the asparagus stalks with a potato peeler if they are rather thick.

2 Tie the stalks together with string or use a wire basket so that they can easily be removed from the pan without damage.

3 Bring a large saucepan of salted water to the boil and plunge in the stalks. Cover with a lid and cook for 4–5 minutes. Pierce one stalk near the base with a sharp knife. If it is fairly soft remove from the heat at once. Do not overcook asparagus or the tender tips will fall off.

4 Drain the asparagus thoroughly and serve on large warm plates with the butter poured over. Both the butter and the asparagus should be warm rather than hot. Serve with the salt and pepper and hand out large napkins!

roasted bell pepper salad

ingredients

SERVES 8
AS PART OF A TAPAS
MEAL

3 red bell peppers

3 yellow bell peppers

5 tbsp Spanish extra-virgin
   olive oil

2 tbsp dry sherry vinegar or
   lemon juice

2 garlic cloves, crushed

pinch of sugar

salt and pepper

1 tbsp capers

8 small black Spanish olives

2 tbsp chopped fresh
   marjoram, plus extra
   sprigs to garnish

method

1 Preheat the broiler. Place the bell peppers on a wire rack or broiler pan and cook under a hot broiler for 10 minutes, until their skins have blackened and blistered, turning them frequently.

2 Remove the roasted bell peppers from the heat, put them in a bowl, and immediately cover tightly with a clean, damp dish towel. Alternatively, you can put the bell peppers in a plastic bag. You will find that the steam helps to soften the skins and makes it easier to remove them. Let the peppers stand for about 15 minutes, until they are cool enough to handle.

3 Holding one bell pepper at a time over a clean bowl, use a sharp knife to make a small hole in the base and gently squeeze out the juices and reserve them. Still holding the bell pepper over the bowl, carefully peel off the blackened skin with your fingers or a knife and discard it. Cut the bell peppers in half and remove the stem, core, and seeds, then cut each bell pepper into neat thin strips. Arrange the bell pepper strips attractively on a serving dish.

4 To the reserved pepper juices add the olive oil, sherry vinegar, garlic, sugar, and salt and pepper to taste. Whisk together until combined. Drizzle the dressing evenly over the salad.

5 Sprinkle the capers, olives, and chopped marjoram over the salad, garnish with marjoram sprigs, and serve at room temperature.

green bean salad with feta cheese

ingredients

SERVES 4

12 oz/350 g green beans

1 red onion, chopped

3–4 tbsp chopped fresh cilantro

2 radishes, thinly sliced

2³/₄ oz/75 g feta cheese
   (drained weight), crumbled

1 tsp chopped fresh oregano,
   plus extra leaves to garnish
   (optional), or ¹/₂ tsp dried

pepper

2 tbsp red wine or fruit vinegar

¹/₃ cup extra-virgin olive oil

3 ripe tomatoes, cut into
   wedges

method

1 Bring about 2 inches/5 cm of water to a boil in the bottom of a steamer. Add the beans to the top part of the steamer, cover, and steam for 5 minutes, or until just tender.

2 Place the beans in a large bowl and add the onion, cilantro, radishes, and feta cheese.

3 Sprinkle the oregano over the salad, then season to taste with pepper. Mix the vinegar and oil together in a small bowl and pour over the salad. Toss gently to mix well.

4 Transfer to a serving platter, surround with the tomato wedges, and serve at once, or cover and chill until ready to serve.

warm red lentil salad with goat cheese

ingredients

SERVES 4

2 tbsp olive oil

2 tsp cumin seeds

2 garlic cloves, crushed

2 tsp grated fresh gingerroot

$1^1/_2$ cups split red lentils

3 cups vegetable stock

2 tbsp chopped fresh mint

2 tbsp chopped fresh cilantro

2 red onions, thinly sliced

$4^3/_8$ cups baby spinach leaves

1 tsp hazelnut oil

$5^1/_2$ oz/150 g soft goat cheese

4 tbsp strained plain yogurt

pepper

1 lemon, cut into quarters,
    to garnish

toasted rye bread, to serve

method

1 Heat half the olive oil in a large pan over medium heat, add the cumin seeds, garlic, and ginger and cook for 2 minutes, stirring constantly.

2 Stir in the lentils, then add the stock, a ladleful at a time, until it is all absorbed, stirring constantly—this will take about 20 minutes. Remove from the heat and stir in the herbs.

3 Meanwhile, heat the remaining olive oil in a skillet over medium heat, add the onions, and cook, stirring frequently, for 10 minutes, or until soft and lightly browned.

4 Toss the spinach in the hazelnut oil in a bowl, then divide between 4 serving plates.

5 Mash the goat cheese with the yogurt in a small bowl and season to taste with pepper.

6 Divide the lentils between the serving plates and top with the onions and goat cheese mixture. Garnish with lemon quarters and serve with toasted rye bread.

mexican three-bean chili stew

ingredients

SERVES 6

generous ¾ cup each dried
   black beans,
cannellini beans and pinto
   beans, soaked
overnight in separate bowls in
   water to cover
2 tbsp olive oil
1 large onion, finely chopped
2 red bell peppers, seeded
   and diced
2 garlic cloves, very finely
   chopped
½ tsp cumin seeds, crushed
1 tsp coriander seeds,
   crushed
1 tsp dried oregano
½–2 tsp chili powder
3 tbsp tomato paste
1 lb 12 oz/800 g canned
   chopped tomatoes
1 tsp sugar
1 tsp salt
2½ cups vegetable stock
3 tbsp chopped fresh cilantro
chopped red onion and
   avocado, to garnish

method

1 Drain the beans, put in separate pans, and cover with cold water. Bring to a boil and boil vigorously for 10–15 minutes, then reduce the heat and let simmer for 35–45 minutes until just tender. Drain and set aside.

2 Heat the oil in a large, heavy-bottom pan over medium heat. Add the onion and bell peppers and cook, stirring frequently, for 5 minutes, or until softened.

3 Add the garlic, cumin, and coriander seeds and oregano and cook, stirring, for 30 seconds until the garlic is beginning to color. Add the chili powder and tomato paste and cook, stirring, for 1 minute. Add the tomatoes, sugar, salt, beans, and stock. Bring to a boil, then reduce the heat, cover, and let simmer, stirring occasionally, for 45 minutes.

4 Stir in the fresh cilantro. Ladle into individual warmed bowls, garnish with the red onion and avocado, and serve immediately.

kidney bean risotto

ingredients

SERVES 4

4 tbsp olive oil

1 onion, chopped

2 garlic cloves, finely chopped

generous $^3/_4$ cup brown rice

$2^1/_2$ cups vegetable stock

1 red bell pepper, seeded and
    chopped

2 celery stalks, sliced

8 oz/225 g cremini
    mushrooms, thinly sliced

15 oz/425 g canned red
    kidney beans, drained
    and rinsed

3 tbsp chopped fresh parsley,
    plus extra to garnish

scant $^3/_8$ cup cashews

salt and pepper

method

1 Heat half the oil in a large, heavy-bottom pan. Add the onion and cook, stirring occasionally, for 5 minutes, or until softened. Add half the garlic and cook, stirring frequently, for 2 minutes, then add the rice and stir for 1 minute, or until the grains are thoroughly coated with the oil.

2 Add the stock and a pinch of salt and bring to a boil, stirring constantly. Reduce the heat, cover, and let simmer for 35–40 minutes, or until all the liquid has been absorbed.

3 Meanwhile, heat the remaining oil in a heavy-bottom skillet. Add the bell pepper and celery and cook, stirring frequently, for 5 minutes. Add the sliced mushrooms and the remaining garlic and cook, stirring frequently, for 4–5 minutes.

4 Stir the rice into the skillet. Add the beans, parsley, and cashews. Season to taste with salt and pepper and cook, stirring constantly, until hot. Transfer to a warmed serving dish, sprinkle with extra parsley, and serve at once.

spinach with chickpeas

ingredients

SERVES 4–6

2 tbsp olive oil

1 large garlic clove, cut in half

1 medium onion, chopped
    finely

$1/2$ tsp cumin

pinch cayenne pepper

pinch turmeric

1 lb 12 oz/800 g canned
    chickpeas, drained
    and rinsed

$1^1/4$ cups baby spinach
    leaves, rinsed and
    shaken dry

2 pimientos del piquillo,
    drained and sliced

salt and pepper

method

1 Heat the oil in a large, lidded skillet over medium-high heat. Add the garlic and cook for 2 minutes, or until golden, but not brown. Remove with a slotted spoon and discard.

2 Add the onion and cumin, cayenne and turmeric and cook, stirring, about 5 minutes until soft. Add the chickpeas and stir round until they are lightly colored with the turmeric and cayenne.

3 Stir in the spinach with just the water clinging to its leaves. Cover and cook for 4–5 minutes until wilted. Uncover, stir in the pimientos del piquillo and continue cooking, stirring gently, until all the liquid evaporates. Season to taste and serve.

vegetable & hazelnut loaf

ingredients

SERVES 4

2 tbsp sunflower-seed oil,
    plus extra for oiling

1 onion, chopped

1 garlic clove, finely chopped

2 celery stalks, chopped

1 tbsp all-purpose flour

scant 1 cup strained canned
    tomatoes

2 cups fresh whole wheat
    bread crumbs

2 carrots, grated

$^3/_4$ cup toasted hazelnuts,
    ground

1 tbsp dark soy sauce

2 tbsp chopped fresh cilantro

1 egg, lightly beaten

salt and pepper

method

1 Preheat the oven to 350°F/180°C. Oil and line a 1-lb/450-g loaf pan. Heat the oil in a heavy-bottom skillet over medium heat. Add the onion and cook, stirring frequently, for 5 minutes, or until softened. Add the garlic and celery and cook, stirring frequently, for 5 minutes. Add the flour and cook, stirring constantly, for 1 minute. Gradually stir in the strained canned tomatoes and cook, stirring constantly, until thickened. Remove the skillet from the heat.

2 Put the bread crumbs, carrots, ground hazelnuts, soy sauce, and cilantro in a bowl. Add the tomato mixture and stir well. Let cool slightly, then beat in the egg and season to taste with salt and pepper.

3 Spoon the mixture into the prepared pan and smooth the surface. Cover with foil and bake in the preheated oven for 1 hour. If serving hot, turn the loaf out on to a warmed serving dish and serve immediately. Alternatively, let cool in the pan before turning out.

vegetarian lasagna

ingredients

SERVES 4

olive oil, for brushing

2 eggplants, sliced

2 tbsp butter

1 garlic clove, finely chopped

4 zucchini, sliced

1 tbsp finely chopped fresh
    flat-leaf parsley

1 tbsp finely chopped fresh
    marjoram

8 oz/225 g mozzarella
    cheese, grated

2$\frac{1}{2}$ cups strained canned
    tomatoes

175 g/6 oz dried no-precook
    lasagna

salt and pepper

2$\frac{1}{2}$ cups Béchamel Sauce

$\frac{1}{2}$ cup freshly grated
    Parmesan cheese

bechamel sauce

1$\frac{1}{4}$ cups milk

1 bay leaf

6 black peppercorns

slice of onion

mace blade

2 tbsp butter

3 tbsp all-purpose flour

salt and pepper

method

1 To make the béchamel sauce, pour the milk into a saucepan. Add the bay leaf, peppercorns, onion and mace. Heat to just below boiling point, then remove from the heat, cover, infuse for 10 minutes, then strain. Melt the butter in a separate saucepan. Sprinkle in the flour and cook over low heat, stirring constantly, for 1 minute. Gradually stir in the milk, then bring to the boil and cook, stirring, until thickened and smooth. Season with salt and pepper.

2 Preheat the oven to 400°F/200°C. Brush a large ovenproof dish with olive oil. Brush a large grill pan with olive oil and heat until smoking. Add half the eggplant slices and cook over medium heat for 8 minutes, or until golden brown all over. Remove the eggplant from the grill pan and drain on paper towels. Add the remaining eggplant slices and extra oil, if necessary, and cook for 8 minutes, or until golden brown all over.

3 Melt the butter in a skillet and add the garlic, zucchini, parsley, and marjoram. Cook over medium heat, stirring frequently, for 5 minutes, or until the zucchini are golden brown all over. Remove from the skillet and let drain on paper towels.

4 Layer the eggplant, zucchini, mozzarella, strained tomatoes, and lasagna in the dish, seasoning with salt and pepper as you go and finishing with a layer of lasagna. Pour over the Béchamel Sauce, making sure that all the pasta is covered. Sprinkle with the grated Parmesan cheese and bake in the preheated oven for 30–40 minutes, or until golden brown. Serve the lasagna immediately.

chili broccoli pasta

ingredients

SERVES 4

8 oz/225 g dried penne or
   macaroni

8 oz/225 g broccoli, cut into
   florets

1/4 cup extra-virgin olive oil

2 large garlic cloves, chopped

2 fresh red chilies, seeded
   and diced

8 cherry tomatoes (optional)

fresh basil leaves, to garnish

method

1 Bring a large pan of salted boiling water to a boil. Add the pasta, return to a boil, and cook for 8–10 minutes until tender but still firm to the bite. Drain the pasta, refresh under cold running water, and drain again. Set aside.

2 Bring a separate pan of salted water to a boil, add the broccoli, and cook for 5 minutes. Drain, refresh under cold running water, and drain again.

3 Heat the oil in the pan that the pasta was cooked in over high heat. Add the garlic, chilies, and tomatoes, if using, and cook, stirring, for 1 minute.

4 Add the broccoli and mix well. Cook for 2 minutes, stirring, to heat through. Add the pasta and mix well again. Cook for an additional minute. Transfer the pasta to a large, warmed serving bowl and serve garnished with basil leaves.

sweet-&-sour vegetables with cashews

ingredients

SERVES 4

1 tbsp vegetable or peanut oil

1 tsp chili oil

2 onions, sliced

2 carrots, thinly sliced

2 zucchini, thinly sliced

4 oz/115 g broccoli,
    cut into florets

4 oz/115 g white mushrooms,
    sliced

4 oz/115 g small bok choy,
    halved

2 tbsp jaggery or brown sugar

2 tbsp Thai soy sauce

1 tbsp rice vinegar

generous $1/3$ cup cashews

method

1 Heat both the oils in a preheated wok or skillet, add the onions, and stir-fry for 1–2 minutes until beginning to soften.

2 Add the carrots, zucchini, and broccoli and stir-fry for 2–3 minutes. Add the mushrooms, bok choy, sugar, soy sauce, and vinegar and stir-fry for 1–2 minutes.

3 Meanwhile, heat a dry, heavy-bottom skillet over high heat, add the cashews, and cook, shaking the skillet frequently, until lightly toasted. Sprinkle the cashews over the stir-fry and serve immediately.

creamy spinach & mushroom pasta

ingredients

SERVES 4

10^1/$_2$ oz/300 g dried
   gluten-free penne or
   pasta of your choice
salt and pepper
2 tbsp olive oil
9 oz/250 g mushrooms, sliced
1 tsp dried oregano
scant 1^1/$_4$ cups vegetable stock
1 tbsp lemon juice
6 tbsp cream cheese
generous 1 cup frozen
   spinach leaves

method

1 Cook the pasta in a large pan of lightly salted boiling water according to the package instructions. Drain, reserving 3/4 cup of the cooking liquid.

2 Meanwhile, heat the oil in a large, heavy-bottom skillet over medium heat, add the mushrooms, and cook, stirring frequently, for 8 minutes, or until almost crisp. Stir in the oregano, stock, and lemon juice and cook for 10–12 minutes, or until the sauce is reduced by half.

3 Stir in the cream cheese and spinach and cook over medium-low heat for 3–5 minutes. Add the reserved cooking liquid, then the cooked pasta. Stir well, season to taste with salt and pepper, and heat through before serving.

roasted garlic creamed potatoes

ingredients

SERVES 4

2 whole garlic bulbs

1 tbsp olive oil

2 lb/900 g mealy potatoes, peeled

1/2 cup milk

2 oz/55 g butter

salt and pepper

method

1 Preheat the oven to 350°F/180°C.

2 Separate the garlic cloves, place on a large piece of foil, and drizzle with the oil. Wrap the garlic in the foil and roast in the oven for about 1 hour, or until very tender. Let cool slightly.

3 Twenty minutes before the end of the cooking time, cut the potatoes into chunks, then cook in a pan of lightly salted boiling water for 15 minutes, or until tender.

4 Meanwhile, squeeze the cooled garlic cloves out of their skins and push through a strainer into a pan. Add the milk, butter, and salt and pepper to taste and heat gently until the butter has melted.

5 Drain the cooked potatoes, then mash in the pan until smooth. Pour in the garlic mixture and heat gently, stirring, until the ingredients are combined. Serve hot.

caramelized onion tart

ingredients

SERVES 4–6

7 tbsp unsalted butter

1 lb 5 oz/600 g onions,
    thinly sliced

2 eggs

generous $1/3$ cup heavy cream

$7/8$ cup grated Gruyère cheese

8-inch/20-cm ready-baked
    pastry shell

$7/8$ cup coarsely grated
    Parmesan cheese

salt and pepper

method

1 Melt the butter in a heavy-bottom skillet over medium heat. Add the onions and cook, stirring frequently to avoid burning, for 30 minutes, or until well-browned and caramelized. Remove the onions from the skillet and set aside.

2 Preheat the oven to 375°F/190°C. Beat the eggs in a large bowl, stir in the cream, and season to taste with salt and pepper. Add the Gruyère and mix well. Stir in the cooked onions.

3 Pour the egg and onion mixture into the baked pastry shell and sprinkle with the Parmesan cheese. Put on a baking sheet. Bake in the preheated oven for 15–20 minutes until the filling has set and begun to brown.

4 Remove from the oven and let rest for at least 10 minutes. The tart can be served hot or left to cool to room temperature.

stir-fried rice with green vegetables

ingredients

SERVES 4

generous 1 cup jasmine rice

2 tbsp. vegetable or peanut oil

1 tbsp. Green Curry Paste

6 scallions, sliced

2 garlic cloves, crushed

1 zucchini, cut into thin sticks

4 oz. yard-long beans

6 oz. asparagus, trimmed

1 tbsp. fish sauce

3–4 fresh Thai basil leaves

method

1 Cook the rice in lightly salted boiling water for 12–15 minutes, drain well, then cool thoroughly and chill overnight.

2 Heat the oil in a wok and stir-fry the curry paste for 1 minute. Add the scallions and garlic and stir-fry for 1 minute.

3 Add the zucchini, beans, and asparagus, and stir-fry for 3–4 minutes, until just tender. Break up the rice and add it to the wok. Cook, stirring constantly for 2–3 minutes, until the rice is hot. Stir in the fish sauce and basil leaves. Serve hot.

greek salad

ingredients

SERVES 4

4 tomatoes, cut into wedges

1 onion, sliced

$^1/_2$ cucumber, sliced

$1^1/_2$ cups kalamata olives,
    stoned

8 oz/225 g feta cheese,
    cubed

2 tbsp fresh cilantro leaves

fresh flat-leaf parsley sprigs,
    to garnish

pita bread, to serve

dressing

5 tbsp extra-virgin olive oil

2 tbsp white wine vinegar

1 tbsp lemon juice

$^1/_2$ tsp sugar

1 tbsp chopped fresh cilantro

salt and pepper

method

1 To make the dressing, put all the ingredients for the dressing into a large bowl and mix well together.

2 Add the tomatoes, onion, cucumber, olives, cheese, and cilantro. Toss all the ingredients together, then divide between individual serving bowls. Garnish with parsley sprigs and serve with pita bread.

stuffed red bell peppers with basil

ingredients

SERVES 4

3/4 cup long-grain
    white or brown rice

4 large red bell peppers

2 tbsp olive oil

1 garlic clove, chopped

4 shallots, chopped

1 celery stalk, chopped

3 tbsp chopped
    toasted walnuts

2 tomatoes, peeled
    and chopped

1 tbsp lemon juice

1/3 cup raisins

4 tbsp freshly grated
    Cheddar cheese

2 tbsp chopped fresh basil

salt and pepper

fresh basil sprigs, to garnish

lemon wedges, to serve

method

1 Preheat the oven to 350°F/180°C. Cook the rice in a pan of lightly salted boiling water for 20 minutes if using white rice, or 35 minutes if using brown. Drain, rinse under cold running water, then drain again.

2 Using a sharp knife, cut the tops off the bell peppers and set aside. Remove the seeds and white cores, then blanch the bell peppers and reserved tops in boiling water for 2 minutes. Remove from the heat and drain well. Heat half the oil in a large skillet. Add the garlic and shallots and cook, stirring, for 3 minutes. Add the celery, walnuts, tomatoes, lemon juice, and raisins and cook for an additional 5 minutes. Remove from the heat and stir in the cheese, chopped basil, and seasoning.

3 Stuff the bell peppers with the rice mixture and arrange them in a baking dish. Place the tops on the bell peppers, drizzle over the remaining oil, loosely cover with foil, and bake in the preheated oven for 45 minutes. Remove from the oven. Garnish with basil sprigs and serve with lemon wedges.

potato-topped vegetables

ingredients

SERVES 4

1 carrot, diced

6 oz/175 g cauliflower florets

6 oz/175 g broccoli florets

1 fennel bulb, sliced

3 oz/85 g green beans, halved

2 tbsp butter

scant $^1/_4$ cup all-purpose flour

$^2/_3$ cup vegetable stock

$^2/_3$ cup dry white wine

$^2/_3$ cup milk

6 oz/175 g cremini
    mushrooms, quartered

2 tbsp chopped fresh sage

topping

2 lb/900 g mealy potatoes,
    diced

2 tbsp butter

4 tbsp plain yogurt

$^5/_8$ cup freshly grated
    Parmesan cheese

1 tsp fennel seeds

salt and pepper

method

1 Preheat the oven to 375°F/190°C. Bring a large pan of water to a boil, add the carrot, cauliflower, broccoli, fennel, and beans and cook for 10 minutes, or until just tender. Drain and set aside.

2 Melt the butter in a pan over low heat, add the flour, and cook, stirring constantly, for 1 minute. Remove from the heat and stir in the stock, wine, and milk. Return to the heat, bring to a boil and cook, stirring constantly, until thickened. Stir in the reserved vegetables, mushrooms, and sage.

3 To make the topping, bring a large pan of water to a boil, add the potatoes, and cook for 10–15 minutes until tender. Drain, return to the pan, and add the butter, yogurt, and half the cheese. Mash with a potato masher or a fork. Stir in the fennel seeds and salt and pepper to taste.

4 Spoon the vegetable mixture into a 4-cup pie dish. Top with the potato mixture. Sprinkle over the remaining cheese. Bake in the preheated oven for 30–35 minutes until golden. Serve immediately.